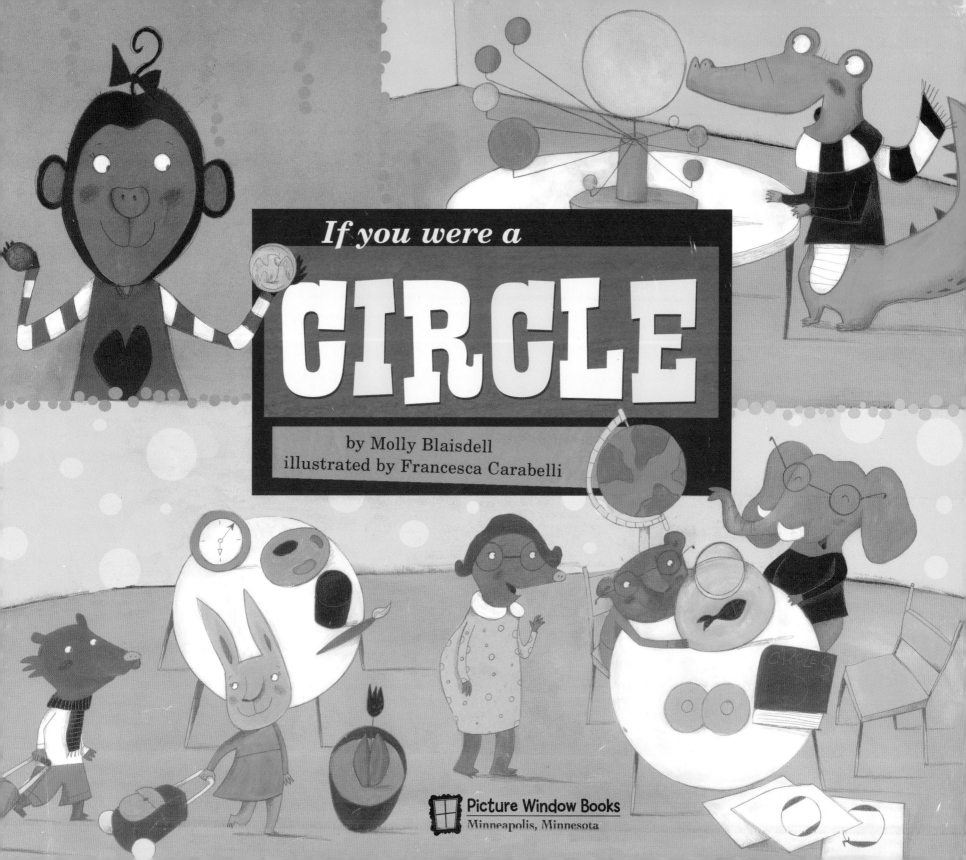

If you were a
CIRCLE

by Molly Blaisdell
illustrated by Francesca Carabelli

Picture Window Books
Minneapolis, Minnesota

Editor: Jill Kalz
Designer: Lori Bye
Page Production: Melissa Kes
Art Director: Nathan Gassman
Editorial Director: Nick Healy
Creative Director: Joe Ewest
The illustrations in this book were created with watercolor and gouache.

Picture Window Books
151 Good Counsel Drive
P.O. Box 669
Mankato, MN 56002-0669
877-845-8392
www.picturewindowbooks.com

Printed in the United States of America.

All books published by Picture Window Books
are manufactured with paper containing
at least 10 percent post-consumer waste.

Library of Congress Cataloging-in-Publication Data
Blaisdell, Molly, 1964-
If you were a circle / by Molly Blaisdell ;
illustrated by Francesca Carabelli.
p. cm. — (Math fun)
Includes index.
ISBN 978-1-4048-5514-4 (library binding)
ISBN 978-1-4048-5686-8 (paperback)
1. Circle—Juvenile literature. 2. Curves—Juvenile literature.
3. Shapes—Juvenile literature. I. Carabelli, Francesca, ill.
II. Title.
QA484.B53 2010
516'.152—dc22
                              2009006888

Special thanks to our
adviser for his expertise:

Stuart Farm, M.Ed.,
Mathematics Lecturer
University of
North Dakota

circle—a closed, curved line made up of all the points that are the same distance from a center point

If you were a circle ...

... you would be a part of the school day.

If you were a circle, you would have no corners or straight lines.

Rita rides her bike to school.

6

Al rides the bus.

ol Bus

Olive's dad drives her to school in the family van.

7

If you were a circle, you would have one curved edge.

Mrs. Mole asks her class to sit down for reading time.

Students sit along
the edge of the rug. 9

If you were a circle, you could be big or small.
But you would always keep your shape.

During math, Olive counts coins.
She stacks quarters, nickels, pennies, and dimes.

If you were a circle, you could be flat.

Rita hands out lemon cookies at snack time.

She puts them on paper plates. Tasty treats!

If you were a circle, you could be the letter O.

Olive's classmates make a birthday card for her. Some write good wishes. Others draw pictures.

If you were a circle, you would have a diameter. A diameter is a straight line that passes through a circle's center and measures the circle's width.

diameter

Mrs. Mole is ready to cut Olive's birthday cake.
First she will cut the cake in half, on the diameter.

If you were a circle, you would have a radius. A radius is a straight line from a circle's center to its edge. The radius is half the length of the diameter.

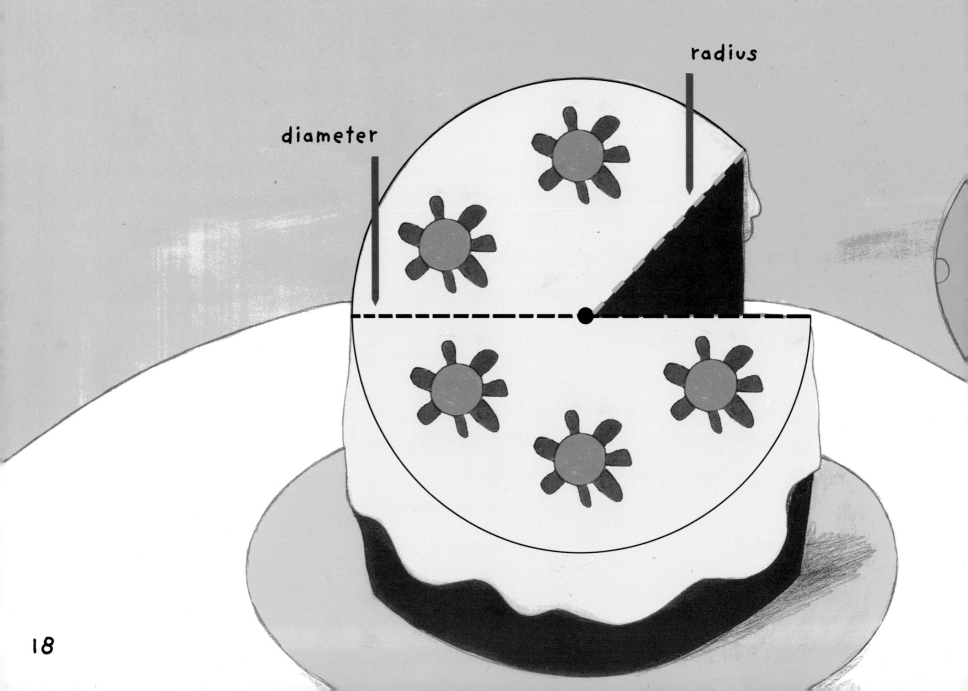

radius

diameter

Mrs. Mole makes sure Olive gets the first piece.
It has the biggest flower on it!

If you were a circle, you could be round, like a ball or globe.
You would be called a sphere.

Today is show-and-tell.
Al brings a model of the solar system.
The sun and planets are spheres.

You would be all around the school, especially at recess ...

... if you were a circle.

FUN WITH CIRCLES

What you need:
a paper plate
at least one friend

What you do:
In turn, hold up the paper plate and pretend that it is a circular object. For example, you might say, "The sun!" Then your friend might say, "A DVD!" Keep playing until one of you can't think of another circular object, or until a minute has passed. Be creative!

Glossary

circle— a closed, curved line made up of all the points that are the same distance from a center point

circular—having a circle shape

diameter—a straight line that passes through a circle's center and measures the circle's width

radius—a straight line from a circle's center to its edge

sphere—a closed, curved surface made up of all the points that are the same distance from a center point

width—the distance from one side of something to the other

To Learn More

More Books to Read

Jones, Christianne C. *Around the Park: A Book About Circles.* Minneapolis: Picture Window Books, 2006.

Olson, Nathan. *Circles Around Town.* Mankato, Minn.: Capstone Press, 2007.

Internet Sites

FactHound offers a safe, fun way to find Internet sites related to this book. All of the sites on FactHound have been researched by our staff.

Here's all you do:
Visit www.facthound.com
FactHound will fetch the best sites for you!

www.FactHound.com

Index

Look for all of the books in the Math Fun series:

If You Were a Circle

If You Were a Divided-by Sign

If You Were a Fraction

If You Were a Minus Sign

If You Were a Minute

If You Were a Plus Sign

If You Were a Polygon

If You Were a Pound or a Kilogram

If You Were a Quadrilateral

If You Were a Quart or a Liter

If You Were a Set

If You Were a Times Sign

If You Were a Triangle

If You Were an Even Number

If You Were an Inch or a Centimeter

If You Were an Odd Number